C000147561

Nautical Wit

summersdale

NAUTICAL WIT

Copyright © Summersdale Publishers Ltd, 2010

Text contributed by Phil Clarke

Illustrations by Kath Walker

Summersdale Publishers Ltd
46 West Street
Chichester
West Sussex
PO19 1RP
UK

www.summersdale.com

Printed and bound in Great Britain

ISBN: 978-1-84953-086-6

Disclaimer
Every effort has been made to attribute the quotations in this collection to the correct source. Should there be any omissions or errors in this respect we apologise and shall be pleased to make the appropriate acknowledgements in any future edition.

Substantial discounts on bulk quantities of Summersdale books are available to corporations, professional associations and other organisations. For details contact Summersdale Publishers by telephone: +44 (0) 1243 771107, fax: +44 (0) 1243 786300 or email: nicky@summersdale.com.

Nautical Wit

Wit

Quips and Quotes for
Seafaring Folk

Richard Benson

Illustrations by Kath Walker

Contents

Editor's Note

Arthur C. Clarke, well known as a science fiction writer and less known as a scuba-diving enthusiast, once said: 'How inappropriate to call this planet Earth when it is clearly Ocean.' That said, despite being creatures most at home on dry land, humans have always found ingenious ways to cope with the watery masses that surround them – for instance, as Sarah Michelle Gellar aptly notes, in the case of a tidal wave hitting LA, one can simply 'grab a fake boob for safety'. There's no denying that the sea has a profound effect on us all, from fanatical fishermen to salty seadogs and from cruise lovers to wave worshippers.

The world has long been flying the flag for all things nautical, and since the time of Noah's ark the wise and witty have had something to say about this majestic pastime. As a whole way of life or simply a weekend pursuit, a spell out on the deep blue sea will broaden your horizons and make you feel swell. So if you're feeling high and dry, batten down the hatches and get to know the ropes with this tome of seafaring quips and quotes that will wipe the stern look from your face and have you booming with laughter in no time!

ALL THINGS BRIGHT
AND BOATIFUL

There is nothing,
absolutely nothing,
half so much
worth doing as
simply messing
about in boats.

Kenneth Grahame

One man on two boats will fall
into the water sooner or later.

Adrian Adam Lee

———◆———

My boat, *Nitchevo*, can sleep
six people who know each other
very well. Or one prude.

Peter Ustinov

———◆———

There are a lot of mysterious things
about boats, such as why anyone
would get on one voluntarily.

P. J. O'Rourke

For a long time I was on a boat
that was so slow we used to forget
what year it was we left port in.

Mark Twain

Wherever you take your
boat, make sure your brain
arrives five minutes earlier.

Anonymous

Boats, like whisky, are all good.

R. D. Culler

No one likes an
ugly boat, however
cheap or fast.

Roger Duncan

A boat is the nearest approach
to a floating, moving, safe bit
of land a man can make.

T. C. Lethbridge

The water is the same on
both sides of the boat.

Finnish proverb

He who has the biggest
boat has right of way.

Anonymous

Let your boat of life be light,
packed with only what you need.

Jerome K. Jerome

———◆———

All boats seem crowded when there
are more than two people aboard.

Anonymous

———◆———

Fortune brings in some boats
that are not steered.

William Shakespeare

There is no single toy Americans
own so many of that they use so
infrequently, as their boats.

Andy Rooney

If a man is to be obsessed by
something, I suppose a boat is
as good as anything, perhaps
a bit better than most.

E. B. White

If you have the sea in your soul,
then boat rides can become
a spiritual experience.

Tom Anderson

My ancestors didn't come over
on the *Mayflower*, but they
were there to meet the boat.

Will Rogers

Nodding the head does
not row the boat.

Irish proverb

SHIP QUIPS

Every ship is a
romantic object,
except that we sail in.

Ralph Waldo Emerson

A great ship asks deep water.

George Herbert

A ship in port is safe, but that's
not what ships are built for.

Grace Murray Hopper

If it's sent by ship then it's a cargo, if
it's sent by road then it's a shipment.

Dave Allen

The irony is that by
the time your ship
comes in you're too
old to enjoy the cruise.

Anonymous

A ship is worse than a gaol.
There is, in a gaol, better
air, better company, better
conveniency of every kind;
and a ship has the additional
disadvantage of being in danger.

Samuel Johnson

———◆———

A community is like a ship:
everyone ought to be
prepared to take the helm.

Henrik Ibsen

When my ship comes
in, I'll be at the airport.

Anonymous

ASHORE THING

It isn't that life
ashore is distasteful
to me. But life at
sea is better.

Sir Francis Drake

Sailors work like horses at sea and spend their money like asses ashore.

Anonymous

Men in a ship are always looking up, and men ashore are usually looking down.

John Masefield

The sure-thing boat never gets far from shore.

Dale Carnegie

Man cannot discover new oceans
unless he has the courage to
lose sight of the shore.

André Gide

———

Praise the sea, on shore remain.

John Florio

———

Hug the shore, let others
try the deep.

Virgil

It's better to be ashore wishing
you were at sea, than at sea
wishing you were ashore.

Anonymous

Help your brother's boat across,
and your own will reach the shore.

Hindu proverb

It's remarkable how quickly a
good and favourable wind can
sweep away the maddening
frustrations of shore living.

Ernest K. Gann

GIVE US A WAVE

I don't know who
named them swells.
There's nothing
swell about them.
They should have
named them awfuls.

Hugo Vihlen

If a tidal wave hits LA just
grab a fake boob for safety.

Sarah Michelle Gellar

If in doubt, stay out to sea. No one
has ever gone aground on a wave.

Anonymous

The breaking of a wave cannot
explain the whole sea.

Vladimir Nabokov

Waves are not
measured in feet
or inches, they
are measured in
increments of fear.

Buzzy Trent

A politician is a person who
can make waves and then
make you think he's the only
one who can save the ship.

Ivern Ball

If you are ever lonely go to the
ocean and the ocean will wave back.

Anonymous

The wind and the waves are always
on the side of the ablest navigator.

Edmund Gibbon

BON VOYAGE

It is not the going out
of port, but the coming
in, that determines the
success of a voyage.

Henry Ward Beecher

If you are contemplating a
voyage and you have the
means, abandon the venture
until your fortunes change.

Sterling Hayden

Voyage upon life's sea,
To yourself be true,
And, whatever your lot may be,
Paddle your own canoe.

Sarah Bolton

To travel hopefully is a
better thing than to arrive.

Robert Louis Stevenson

The great difference between
voyages rests not with the ships, but
with the people you meet on them.

Amelia E. Barr

If Columbus had had an
advisory committee he would
probably still be at the dock.

Arthur J. Goldberg

The journey of a thousand
miles begins with a broken main
halyard and a leaky toilet valve.

Anonymous

Make voyages! Attempt them.
There's nothing else.

Tennessee Williams

◆

To young men contemplating
a voyage I would say go.

Joshua Slocum

A YARDARM
AND A LEG

Anyone who has to
ask about the annual
upkeep of a yacht
can't afford one.

J. P. Morgan

Give a man a fish, he eats for
a day. Give a man a boat, he
cannot afford to eat again.

Anonymous

———

Money can't buy you happiness.
But it can buy you a yacht big
enough to pull up right alongside it.

David Lee Roth

To marry a wife will
cost you much trouble;
But to fit out a
ship the expenses
are double!

Bill Tilman

Don't buy the biggest boat
you can afford; buy the smallest
one you can live with.

Anonymous

———

People with the boat bug are never
happier than when they are poking
around marinas, fantasising about
owning other people's boats.

Randy Wayne White

GOOD TIDE-INGS

Only when the tide goes out do you discover who's been swimming naked.

Warren Buffett

She ate so many clams that her
stomach rose and fell with the tide.

Louis Kronenberger

———◆———

Good luck comes in slender
currents, misfortune in a rolling tide.

Irish proverb

———◆———

Never go into strange places on
a falling tide without a pilot.

Thomas Gibson Bowles

You cannot hold back a good laugh any more than you can the tide. Both are forces of nature.

William Rotsler

The tide makes no difference to a sunken ship.

Anonymous

Some lives are like an ebbing tide in a harbour; the farther they go out, the more mud they expose.

Austin O'Malley

HELLO SAILOR!

If life is a marriage,
then a sailor's life is a
series of honeymoons.

David Baboulene

Why do sailors love the sea?
Because without it they would
have to carry their boats.

Anonymous

How happy is the sailor's life,
from coast to coast to roam;
In every port he finds a wife,
in every land a home.

Isaac Bickerstaffe

Sailors, with their built-in sense
of order, service and discipline,
should really be running the world.

Nicholas Monsarrat

Without patience, a sailor
I would never be.

Lee Allred

A sailor is an artist whose
medium is the wind.

Webb Chiles

We be three poor mariners,
Newly come from the seas,
We spend our lives in jeopardy
While others live at ease.

Seventeenth-century sea shanty

The Ancient Mariner would
not have taken so well if it had
been called *The Old Sailor*.

Samuel Butler

A smooth sea never made
a skilled mariner.

English proverb

———

A woman knows the face of
the man she loves as a sailor
knows the open sea.

Honoré de Balzac

———

When men come to like a sea-life,
they are not fit to live on land.

Samuel Johnson

Why do opera singers
make good sailors?
Because they can handle
the high seas.

Anonymous

A tourist remains an outsider
throughout his visit; but a sailor
is part of the local scene from
the moment he arrives.

Anne Davison

A sailor's joys are as
simple as a child's.

Bernard Moitessier

—•—

You are not a fully fledged sailor
unless you have sailed under full sail.

Irish proverb

—•—

Prevention is, as in other aspects
of seamanship, better than cure.

Robin Knox-Johnston

The art of the
sailor is to leave
nothing to chance.

Annie Van de Wiele

SEAFOOD FOR THOUGHT

Fish is the only food that is considered spoiled once it smells like what it is.

P. J. O'Rourke

Bad cooking is responsible
for more trouble at sea than all
other things put together.

Thomas Fleming Day

Our oceans are getting so polluted,
the other day I caught a tuna fish
that was already packed in oil.

Charlie Viracola

I'm on a seafood diet.
I see food and I eat it.

Les Dawson

Fish, to taste good, must swim three times: in water, in butter and in wine.

Polish proverb

Life is rather like a tin of sardines, we're all of us looking for the key.

Alan Bennett

Fish and visitors smell in three days.

Benjamin Franklin

I believe that lobsters are the result of a terrible genetic accident involving nuclear radiation and cockroaches.

Dave Barry

———❦———

Why does Sea World have a seafood restaurant? I'm halfway through my fish burger [thinking] I could be eating a slow learner.

Lynda Montgomery

If it swims, it's edible.

Bill Demmond

⬥

You know why fish are so
thin? They eat fish.

Jerry Seinfeld

⬥

Oysters are the most tender and
delicate of all seafoods. They
stay in bed all day and night.

Hector Bolitho

ON COURSE?
OF COURSE!

Navigation is easy.
If it wasn't they
wouldn't be able to
teach it to sailors.

James Lawrence

They were all fine sailing days, but
unfortunately they were ideal only
for sailing in the wrong direction.

Francis Brenton

Navigation is what tells you where
you are, even when you aren't.

Anonymous

One who in a crisis forgets
nautical language and shouts:
'For God's sake turn left!'

Michael Green on coarse sailors

Set your course by the stars, not
by the lights of every passing ship.

General Omar Bradley

There are no signposts in the sea.

Dave Collins

The rules of navigation
never navigated a ship.

Thomas Reid

Journeys, as I've said before,
are in the mind, not on maps.

Steve Haywood

TERMS OF SAIL

No more expensive
way of going really
slowly has been
invented by man
than sailing.

Gary Mull

Sailing is like being a child
again: wide eyes, big smile
and a soggy bottom.

Anonymous

❧

He was now convinced that the most
valuable sail on board was the diesel.

Ray Kauffman

The pessimist complains about
the wind; the optimist expects it to
change; the realist adjusts the sails.

William Arthur Ward

The goal is not to sail the boat,
but rather to help the
boat sail herself.

John Rousmaniere

Raise your sail one foot, and
you get ten feet of wind.

Chinese proverb

❖

Sailing: the fine art of getting
wet and becoming ill while slowly
going nowhere at great expense.

Anonymous

❖

The days pass happily with
me wherever my ship sails.

Joshua Slocum

Any fool can carry
on, but a wise
man knows how to
shorten sail in time.

Joseph Conrad

SEASICK AS A PARROT

If it was not for
seasickness, the whole
world would be sailors.

Charles Darwin

Seasickness is a condition
which is never helped by sherry,
but always helped by port.

Anonymous

One of the best temporary
cures for pride and affection is
seasickness; a man who wants
to vomit never puts on airs.

Josh Billings

To cure seasickness,
find a good big oak
tree and wrap your
arms around it.

Samuel Johnson

Seasickness is the only thing
that can make a tourist look like
his passport photograph.

Anonymous

—◆—

If there is one thing in the world
that will make a man peculiarly and
insufferably self-conceited, it is
to have his stomach behave itself
the first day at sea, when nearly
all his comrades are seasick.

Mark Twain

I was so seasick, my stomach was ejecting meals I had hoped to eat the following week.

Fred Allen

Jumping into the sea is a
certain cure for seasickness.

John Ruskin

Its not the size of the ship
that makes you seasick, it's
the motion of the ocean.

Joy Sutton on what her grandmother used to say

AYE AYE OF THE STORM

I once knew a writer
who, after saying
beautiful things about
the sea, passed
through a Pacific
hurricane, and he
became a changed man.

Joshua Slocum

No one would ever have crossed
the ocean if he could have gotten
off the ship in the storm.

Charles Kettering

The only safe ship in a
storm is leadership.

Faye Wattleton

The world isn't interested in the
storms you encountered, but whether
or not you brought in the ship.

Raul Armesto

Sailors get to know each other
better when there is a storm.

French proverb

The good seaman weathers the
storm he cannot avoid, and avoids
the storm he cannot weather.

Anonymous

I hate storms, but calms
undermine my spirits.

Bernard Moitessier

It is better to meet danger than
to wait for it. He that is on a lee
shore, and foresees a hurricane,
stands out to sea and encounters
a storm to avoid a shipwreck.

Charles Caleb Colton

We are all in the same boat in
a stormy sea, and we owe each
other a terrible loyalty.

G. K. Chesterton

THE DRUNKEN SAILOR

Any damn fool can
navigate the world
sober. It takes a
really good sailor
to do it drunk.

Sir Francis Chichester

I'd rather be in a boat with a drink on the rocks, than in the drink with a boat on the rocks.

Anonymous

In Western Australia they don't even know how to make that vital piece of sailing boat equipment, the gin and tonic.

P. J. O'Rourke

And Noah he often said to his
wife when he sat down to dine,
'I don't care where the water goes
if it doesn't get into the wine'.

G. K. Chesterton

The passenger on a cruise who
doesn't know port from starboard
should look at the label on the bottle.

Anonymous

I want a boat that drinks six,
eats four, and sleeps two.

Ernest K. Gann

Wine hath drowned more
men than the sea.

Thomas Fuller

Give [a man] a fishing lesson
and he'll sit in a boat drinking
beer every weekend.

Alex Blackwell

To the question,
'When were your
spirits at the lowest
ebb?' the obvious
answer seemed
to be, 'When the
gin gave out.'

Sir Francis Chichester

CONTEMPLATING ONE'S NAVAL

My only great
qualification for being
put at the head of
the Navy is that I am
very much at sea.

Edward Carson

Don't talk to me about naval tradition. It's nothing but rum, sodomy and the lash.

Winston Churchill

You clean up, get a haircut, buy new clothes and any important information will be given to you strictly on a need-to-know basis.

Anonymous on the similarities between getting a new girlfriend and joining the Navy

Obesity is now a
problem in the navy.
They've created
a new rank: Really
Big Rear Admiral.

Jay Leno

Why does the new Italian Navy
have glass bottom boats? To
see the old Italian Navy!

Henny Youngman

❦

The only difference between
prison and a ship at sea in the
Navy is prisoners generally have
more hot water and space!

Rich Slayden

DANGEROUS WATERS

The mark of a great
shiphandler is never
getting into situations
that require great
shiphandling.

Ernest J. King

If you wish to avoid foreign collision,
you had better abandon the ocean.

Henry Clay

❦

Remember the first rule of boating
safety: stay away from water.

Anonymous

❦

I'm afraid of sharks, but only
in a water situation.

Demetri Martin

In certain places, at certain
hours, gazing at the sea is
dangerous. It is what looking
at a woman sometimes is.

Victor Hugo

You don't have to swim faster
than the shark, just faster
than the guy next to you.

Peter Benchley

I was at sea the other day
and loads of meat floated
past. It was a bit choppy.

Tim Vine

He that will not sail till all dangers
are over must never put to sea.

Thomas Fuller

A collision at sea can
ruin your whole day.

Attributed to Thucydides

I scream the same way whether I'm about to be devoured by a Great White or if a piece of seaweed touches my foot.

Axel Rose

❦

Only two sailors, in my experience, never ran aground. One never left port and the other was an atrocious liar.

Don Bamford

Did you hear about the ship that
ran aground carrying a cargo
of red and black paints? The
whole crew was marooned.

Anonymous

━━━◆━━━

If I were shipwrecked, and could
only have one book, what would
it be?... 'How to Build a Boat'.

Steven Wright

He who lets the sea
lull him into a false
sense of security is in
very grave danger.

Hammond Innes

AT THE
CAPTAIN'S TABLE

If the highest aim of
a captain were to
preserve his ship,
he would keep it
in port forever.

St Thomas Aquinas

We call him 'Skipper', not because
of his nautical knowledge, but
because of how many payments
he's missed on his boat.

Anonymous

———◆———

Leadership is like the old galley
ships. Hundreds are rowing,
but only one (the captain)
knows where they are going.

Anonymous

When I lost my rifle, the Army charged me eighty-five dollars. That is why in the Navy the Captain goes down with the ship.

Dick Gregory

In this country it's a good thing
to kill an admiral now and then
to encourage the others.

Voltaire

No captain can do very
wrong if he places his ship
alongside that of the enemy.

Horatio Nelson

FLOODY HELL

I don't believe Noah
could have rounded up
all the animals in one
herd without the skunk
causing a stampede.

Will Rogers

When the earth floods from
global warming, the swimmers
will rule the world.

Anonymous

The only thing that stops God
from sending another flood is
that the first one was useless.

Nicholas Chamfort

Noah was a brave man
to sail in a wooden
boat with two termites.

Anonymous

Nothing is wrong
with California that
a rise in the ocean
level wouldn't cure.

Ross MacDonald

JUST CRUISING

I entertained on a
cruising trip that
was so much fun
that I had to sink my
yacht to make my
guests go home.

F. Scott Fitzgerald

If you have to be somewhere
by a certain date, you aren't
cruising, you're racing.

Anonymous

———•———

Cruising sailors make lists like
stagnant water makes mosquitoes.

Reese Palley

———•———

Cruisers don't have
plans, just intentions.

Anonymous

The lovely thing about cruising
is that planning usually turns
out to be of little use.

Dom Degnon

During a cruise a man never
runs out of money as fast as
his wife runs out of clothes.

Anonymous

Old and young, we are
all on our last cruise.

Robert Louis Stevenson

We were victims of the beginning
cruiser's syndrome – a pervading
sense that cruising meant moving.

Jim Moore

One is to go out in wider waters
from a sheltered place. The
other is to go into a sheltered
place from wider waters.

Howard Bloomfield on the pleasures of cruising

GET KNOTTED

A good knot on a
bad rope is no better
than a bad knot.

Alvin Smith

To be always ready a man
must be able to cut a knot, for
everything cannot be untied.

Henri Frédéric Amiel

It is infinitely easier to shake out a
reef when one is bored, than it is to
try to tie one in when one is scared.

Anonymous

Life is too short to splice wire rope.

Bernard Moitessier

When you reach the
end of your rope, tie a
knot in it and hang on.

Thomas Jefferson

We learn the rope of life
by untying its knots.

Jean Toomer

Skipper: This boat makes
twenty five knots per hour.
Passenger: How long does it
take your men to untie them?

Anonymous

Do not be in a hurry to tie
what you cannot untie.

English proverb

The first lesson a yachtsman
should learn is to join the ropes
together, sailor fashion.

Anonymous

In splicing, practice makes
perfect, and in the doing you
will learn more than from reading
any ten books on the subject.

Hervey Garrett Smith

FISHING LINES

Good fishing is just
a matter of timing.
You have to get
there yesterday.

Milton Berle

There's a fine line between
fishing and just standing on
the shore like an idiot.

Steven Wright

The art of fishing is sitting
still for a long time until you
don't catch anything.

Anonymous

Many men go fishing all of their
lives without knowing that it
is not fish they are after.

Henry David Thoreau

Fishing is a jerk
on one end of the
line waiting for a
jerk on the other
end of the line.

Mark Twain

Nothing makes a fish bigger
than almost being caught.

Anonymous

My biggest worry is that my wife
(when I'm dead) will sell my fishing
gear for what I said I paid for it.

Koos Brandt

The fishermen know that the sea is dangerous and the storm terrible, but they have never found these dangers sufficient reason for remaining ashore.

Vincent Van Gogh

All fishermen are liars; it's an occupational disease with them like housemaid's knee or editor's ulcers.

Beatrice Cook

Believe me, a group of fishermen walking up the towpath is worse than the Army on manoeuvres.

Steve Haywood

Of all the liars among mankind, the fisherman is the most trustworthy.

William Sherwood Fox

Only a fisherman thinks it's worth spending one hundred dollars for a fishing outfit to catch one dollar's worth of fish.

Anonymous

NOT WAVING BUT DROWNING

You don't drown
by falling in the
water. You drown
by staying in there.

Edwin Louis Cole

He who has not yet reached the
opposite shore should not make
fun of him who is drowning.

Guinean proverb

—◆—

A friend of mine drowned in
a bowl of muesli. A strong
currant pulled him in.

Tommy Cooper

—◆—

No man drowns if he perseveres
in praying to God, and can swim.

Russian proverb

It was as helpful as throwing a
drowning man both ends of the rope.

Arthur Baer

While sinking to the bottom of a lake
or ocean, screaming does not help.

Anonymous

It is a mistake that there is no bath
that will cure people's manners
but drowning would help.

Mark Twain

If one synchronised swimmer drowns,
do all the rest have to drown too?

Steven Wright

❦

If a man is destined to drown, he will
drown even in a spoonful of water.

Yiddish proverb

❦

When a man is between the devil
and the deep blue sea, his fear
of drowning generally triumphs.

Anonymous

One never dives into the water to
save a drowning man more eagerly
than when there are others present.

Friedrich Nietzsche

❦

If you wish to drown do not torture
yourself with shallow water.

Bulgarian proverb

OCEAN ONE-LINERS

Ocean: a body of
water occupying
about two-thirds of
a world made for man
– who has no gills.

Ambrose Bierce

An ocean liner is a night club
and swimming pool that also
crosses the high seas.

Anonymous

An ocean liner is a night club
and swimming pool that also
crosses the high seas.

Anonymous

How inappropriate to call this planet
Earth when it is quite clearly Ocean.

Arthur C. Clarke

He who crosses the ocean
twice without taking a bath
is a dirty double-crosser.

Anonymous

❧

Geniuses are like ocean liners:
they should never meet.

Louis Aragon

A LITTLE CRAFTY

Vessels large may
venture more,
But little boats should
keep near shore.

Benjamin Franklin

Other places do seem so cramped
up and smothery, but a raft don't.
You feel mighty free and easy
and comfortable on a raft.

Mark Twain

A small craft in an ocean is, or
should be, a benevolent dictatorship.

Tristan Jones

God is good but never
dance in a small boat.

Irish proverb

A small boat and a suitcase
full of money beats a 40-footer
tied to the bank every time.

Anonymous

When a large vessel has
opened a way it is easy for
a small one to follow.

Chinese proverb

WALKING THE PLANK

Why join the Navy if
you can be a pirate?

Steve Jobs

Now and then we had a hope that
if we lived and were good, God
would permit us to be pirates.

Mark Twain

Why are pirates pirates?
Cos they Arrrrrr!

Anonymous

It is when pirates count their booty
that they become mere thieves.

William Bolitho

How do pirates navigate their ships?
With the staaarrs!

Anonymous

❦

Both are ways to make a
good, dishonest living.

Keith Richards on being a rock star and a pirate

❦

The existence of the sea means
the existence of pirates.

Malayan proverb

How did Captain
Hook die?
He wiped with
the wrong hand.

Tommy Sledge

How much does the pirate
pay for an ear-piercing?
A buccaneer!

Anonymous

The average man will bristle if
you say his father was dishonest,
but he will brag a little if... his
great-grandfather was a pirate.

Bern Williams

What do you call
1,000 pirates
in a room?
Avast conspiracy!

Anonymous

RELATION SHIPS

My wife and I went
to a hotel where
we got a waterbed.
My wife called it
the Dead Sea.

Henny Youngman

When it comes to exploring the
sea of love, I prefer buoys.

Andrew G. Dehel

—◆—

Matrimony: the high sea for which
no compass has yet been invented.

Heinrich Heine

—◆—

Sigh no more, ladies, sigh no more,
Men were deceivers ever,
One foot in sea and one on shore,
To one thing constant never.

William Shakespeare

Marriage may often be a stormy lake, but celibacy is almost always a muddy horse pond.

Thomas Love Peacock

It wasn't long before we tied the knot. No, I don't mean we got married. Our commitment to each other was far more enduring than this. What I mean is we bought our first boat together.

Steve Haywood

Friendship is a ship big enough
to carry two in fair weather,
but only one in foul.

Ambrose Bierce

Honolulu – it's got everything.
Sand for the children, sun for the
wife, sharks for the wife's mother.

Ken Dodd

SURF'S UP

I tried body-surfing
once, but how often
do you find a corpse?

Emo Philips

Neither can the wave that has passed by be recalled, nor the hour which has passed return again.

Ovid

———————

When the waves start pushing ten feet, I get this tremendous urge to make a sandwich.

Bruce Jenkins

Boardshorts – the
one piece of clothing
that epitomises
the freedom of
surf culture.

Tom Anderson

It's like the mafia. Once you're in –
you're in. There's no getting out.

Kelly Slater on surfing

❧

The hardest part of surfing big
waves is getting off the beach.

Anonymous

❧

Surfing is very much like making
love. It always feels good, no matter
how many times you've done it.

Paul Strauch

We were brothers and
sisters, weren't we:
the shoeless, jobless
tribe of nature lovers
against the slick 4x4s
and comfort cars
of rich America.

Tom Anderson on surfers

SHIPWRIGHTS
AND WRONGS

Ships are the nearest
things to dreams that
hands have ever made.

Robert N. Rose

You are not going to find the ideal
boat. You are not even going to
have it if you design it from scratch.

Carl Lane

What do we get when we
plant the tree?
We plant the ship which
will cross the sea.

Henry Abbey

Of all the things that man has made...
none possesses so distinct a life
and character of its own, as a ship.

Henry van Dyke

———•———

The end stages of Boat Building
Disease can make a strong man cry.

Gary Frankel

DEEP TROUBLE

Sponges grow in the ocean... I wonder how much deeper the ocean would be if that didn't happen?

Steven Wright

Shallow's where a
lamb could wade and
depth's where an
elephant would drown.

Mathew Henry

It is best for the mariner, if he
can manage it, not to think too
deeply during times of stress.

Ralph Stock

I worked as a deep-sea diver once.
I couldn't stand the pressure.

Tim Vine

A good time to keep your mouth
shut is when you're in deep water.

Sidney Goff

SWIMMIN' WITH WOMEN

I much prefer travelling
in non-British ships.
There is none
of that nonsense
about women and
children first.

W. Somerset Maugham

Seize the moment.
Remember all those
women on the *Titanic*
who waved off the
dessert cart.

Erma Bombeck

I have often wanted to drown
my troubles, but I can't get
my wife to go swimming.

Jimmy Carter

❧

Time and tide wait for no man, but
always stand still for a woman of 30.

Robert Frost

❧

I could never learn to like her
– except on a raft at sea with
no other provisions in sight.

Mark Twain

Approaching a dock with a boat
it is like approaching a woman
in a bar; very seldom is a slow
approach a poor approach.

Anonymous

Red dress in morning,
sailors take warning.

Sterling Hayden

If a sailor had a wife in every port,
he'd also have a wife in every court.

Anonymous

The man who has
a girl in every port
is not a sailor but
a wholesaler.

Evan Esar

THAT SINKING
FEELING

It is not the ship in the
water but the water in
the ship that sinks it.

J. Wilbur Chapman

Nervous first-timer to skipper: Do yachts like this sink very often? Skipper: No, usually it's only once!

Anonymous

———

Beware of little expenses; a small leak will sink a great ship.

Benjamin Franklin

———

Two captains will sink the ship.

Turkish proverb

It is cheering to see that the rats are still around – the ship is not sinking.

Eric Hoffer

⬩—⬩

When the ship has sunk
everyone knows how she
might have been saved.

Italian proverb

⬩—⬩

Some ships are designed to sink...
others require our assistance.

Nathan Zelk

Always stand up in the boat so you'll
have a good view when it capsizes.

Anonymous

———

What did I think of *Titanic*?
I'd rather have been on it.

Miles Kruger

———

You cannot sink someone
else's end of the boat and
still keep your own afloat.

Charles Bower

Should you
find yourself in a
chronically leaking
boat... changing
vessels is likely to
be more productive
than... patching leaks.

Warren Buffett

A WHALE OF A TIME

It would have approached nearer to the idea of a miracle if Jonah had swallowed the whale.

Thomas Paine

If swimming is so good for your
figure, how do you explain whales?

Anonymous

❖

A whale is harpooned
only when it spouts.

Henry Hillman

❖

Jonah proved that you can't
keep a good man down.

Anonymous

175

Confidence is going
after Moby Dick
in a rowboat, and
taking the tartar
sauce with you.

Zig Ziglar

Consider the whale: it never gets into trouble until it starts spouting.

Anonymous

———•———

When you get cheated by a shark, think of Jonah: he was completely taken in by a whale.

Anonymous

NAUTICAL BUT NICE

The transatlantic
crossing was so
rough that the only
thing I could keep
on my stomach was
the first mate.

Dorothy Parker

Sailing is like screwing; you
can never get enough.

Brigitte Bardot

May the wind be behind you
and may it not be your own.

Anonymous

A lot of people attack the
sea, I make love to it.

Jacques Cousteau

In rough and rolling
seas all good
sailors sit to pee.

Anonymous

THE HOLY SEA

Sailors ought never
to go to church.
They ought to go to
hell, where it is much
more comfortable.

H. G. Wells

Lighthouses are more
helpful than churches.

Benjamin Franklin

❦

Below 40° south there is no law,
Below 50° south there is no God.

Old sailors' proverb

❦

When I forget how talented
God is, I look to the sea.

Whoopi Goldberg

The true peace of God begins at any spot a thousand miles from the nearest land.

Joseph Conrad

Sometimes God calms the storm.
At other times, He calms the sailor.
And sometimes He makes us swim.

Anonymous

One might better try to sail the
Atlantic in a paper boat than try
to get to heaven on good works.

Charles H. Spurgeon

SOMETHING FISHY

Fish must be brain food, because they travel in schools.

Anonymous

No wise fish would
go anywhere without
a porpoise.

Lewis Carroll

If you're a fish, and you want
to be a fish stick, you must
have very good posture.

Mitch Hedberg

———

Very few fish can close their eyes,
but then the sea is never dusty.

Anonymous

I never drink water because of the
disgusting things that fish do in it.

W. C. Fields

Never forget that only dead
fish swim with the stream.

Malcolm Muggeridge

UNDER THE WEATHER

Off Cape Horn
there are but two
kinds of weather,
neither one of them
a pleasant kind.

John Masefield

There is no such thing as bad
weather, only bad clothes.

Norwegian proverb

Not that I have learned to feel
secure in the fog, but at least I have
learned how to grope without panic.

Herb Payson

Climate is what you expect,
weather is what you get.

Robert A. Heinlein

When fog descends, the anchor
is a navigational aid: it finds you a
place where you are not sinking!

Gene Walker

Being hove to in a long gale
is the most boring way of
being terrified I know.

Donald Hamilton

Mackerel skies and mares' tails,
soon will be time to shorten sails.

Old sailors' proverb

Whether the weather be hot,
Or whether the weather be not,
We'll weather the weather,
whatever the weather,
Whether we like it or not.

British school rhyme

For one thing, I was no longer
alone; a man is never alone with the
wind – and the boat made three.

Hilaire Belloc

Wind to a sailor is what
money is to life on shore.

Sterling Hayden

UTTERLY
LANDLUBBERLY

I've never seen the
point of the sea,
except where it
meets the land.

Alan Bennett

Extremely foolish advice is likely to
be uttered by those who are looking
at the labouring vessel from the land.

Arthur Helps

I've had it. If anyone sees me
near a boat they can shoot me.

Steve Redgrave

Love the sea? I
dote upon it –
from the beach.

Douglas Jerrold

Son, you have to remember
that people like terra firma – the
more firma, the less terra.

Sid Bryant

The wonder is always new that
any sane man can be a sailor.

Ralph Waldo Emerson

That packet of assorted
miseries which we call a ship.

Rudyard Kipling

Coarse sailing is not mucking
around in boats, but boating
around in muck.

Michael Green

SEA-ING THINGS

When I was a boy
the Dead Sea
was only sick.

George Burns

The cure for anything is salt
water; sweat, tears or the sea.

Isak Dinesen

———•———

The sea finds out everything
you did wrong.

Francis Stokes

———•———

The sea, once it casts its spell, holds
one in its net of wonder forever.

Jacques Cousteau

Those who live by the sea can
hardly form a single thought of
which the sea would not be part.

Hermann Broch

❦

At sea, I learned how little a
person needs, not how much.

Robin Lee Graham

❦

I wanted freedom, open air and
adventure. I found it on the sea.

Alain Gerbault

The sea is the same as it
has been since before men
ever went on it in boats.

Ernest Hemingway

The sea hates a coward.

Eugene O'Neill

Whenever your preparations for
the sea are poor; the sea worms
its way in and finds the problems.

Francis Stokes

Anyone can hold the helm
when the sea is calm.

Publilius Syrus

The sea drives truth
into a man like salt.

Hilaire Belloc

It's out there at sea that
you are really yourself.

Vito Dumas

There is nothing
more enticing,
disenchanting,
and enslaving than
the life at sea.

Joseph Conrad

Have you enjoyed this book?
If so, why not write a review
on your favourite website?

Thanks very much for buying
this Summersdale book.

www.summersdale.com